# How To Overcome Workplace Toxicity And Dysfunction

*Step-by-Step Guide For Recognizing, Responding and Reclaiming Control*

By

Jennifer Govers

**Copyright © 2024 Jennifer Govers**

All rights reserved. No part of this publication may be reproduced, distributed, or transmitted in any form or by any means, including photocopying, recording, or other electronic or mechanical methods, without the prior written permission of the publisher, except in the case of brief quotations embodied in critical reviews and certain other noncommercial uses permitted by copyright law.

This book is a work of fiction. Names, characters, places, and incidents are products of the Author's imagination or are used fictitiously. Any resemblance to actual events or locales or persons, living or dead, is entirely coincidental.

# Table of Contents

Introduction ................................................................. 6
   Traversing the Toxic Landscape ................................. 6

Chapter 1 .................................................................. 10
   Recognizing Toxicity: Deciphering Indications and Symptoms ................................................................. 10
      Identifying Toxic Conduct and Environments ............. 11
      Impact on Mental Health and Productivity ................. 13
      Case Studies: Exemplifying Varied Forms of Workplace Toxicity ............................................................... 17

Chapter 2 .................................................................. 24
   Responding to Dysfunction: Effective Strategies for Confrontation ............................................................ 24
      Communication Techniques for Dealing with Toxic Behavior ................................................................ 27
      Establishing Limits and Standing Up for Yourself ....... 31
      Finding Assistance: Allies and Resources for Managing Toxicity ............................................................... 36

Chapter 3 .................................................................. 42
   Regaining Authority: Taking Steps Towards a Healthier Workplace ............................................................... 42
      Cultivating Resilience: Coping Mechanisms for Managing Toxicity .................................................... 47

    Advocating for Change: Initiating Dialogues and Actions for Improvement ....................................................... 51

    Legal Considerations: Grasping Rights and Recourse Options ................................................................................ 55

Chapter 4 ................................................................................ 60

    Promoting Positive Transformation: Building a Healthy Work Environment ....................................................... 60

    The Role of Leadership in Addressing and Preempting Workplace Toxicity ................................................. 62

    Strategies for Revitalizing Workplace Environments to Foster Teamwork and Excellence .............................. 65

    Maintaining Momentum: Ensuring Long-Term Viability of a Positive Work Environment ................................ 71

Conclusion ............................................................................. 77

# Introduction

**Traversing the Toxic Landscape**

In today's rapidly evolving work settings, maneuvering through the complexities of the modern workplace can often resemble navigating a hazardous terrain. The indicators of toxicity aren't always overt; they can subtly permeate our surroundings, manifesting in diverse forms, impacting our well-being and effectiveness, and leaving us feeling depleted, demoralized, and disconnected.

However, recognizing these signals necessitates heightened awareness. By comprehending the behaviors and dynamics fueling toxicity, we enhance our ability to detect them when they surface. Whether it's micromanagement, harassment, or fostering a culture of intimidation, identifying the warning signs serves as the initial stride toward regaining authority over our work environment.

Furthermore, the repercussions of toxicity extend beyond individual distress; they significantly impede organizational performance. Elevated turnover rates, diminished morale, and escalated conflicts collectively contribute to a toxic work culture that ultimately undermines productivity and innovation. Acknowledging these ramifications underscores the urgency of proactively addressing toxicity.

Throughout this manuscript, we'll examine the intricacies of workplace toxicity, studying its multifaceted manifestations and offering pragmatic approaches for efficacious responses. By empowering individuals to discern, address, and ultimately reclaim control in toxic work atmospheres, our objective is to cultivate more robust, productive workplaces for all.

# Chapter 1

## Recognizing Toxicity: Deciphering Indications and Symptoms

In the pursuit of cultivating healthier work environments, grasping the cues and manifestations of toxicity is paramount. Toxic conduct can manifest in various guises, from nuanced forms of manipulation and passive aggression to outright hostility and harassment. Recognizing these behaviors at an early stage is crucial, as they often intensify over time, fostering a toxic ambiance that infiltrates the entire workplace. Indicators may encompass excessive gossiping, recurrent blame-shifting, or a pervasive lack of accountability among team members. Additionally, toxic environments often thrive on power differentials and hierarchical structures, where select individuals wield disproportionate influence, exploiting their positions for personal benefit or to undermine others. By refining our ability to discern these signs and symptoms, we empower ourselves to proactively address toxicity and prevent its corrosive impact from spreading further.

## Identifying Toxic Conduct and Environments

The journey demands a refined comprehension of human interaction and organizational dynamics. It's not always as straightforward as pinpointing clear acts of aggression or hostility; oftentimes, toxicity manifests in subtle ways that may go unnoticed. For instance, passive-aggressive remarks, covert undermining of colleagues, or indulging in gossip might initially seem innocuous, yet they can gradually erode trust and foster a culture of toxicity within teams and departments.

Moreover, toxic environments frequently thrive on power imbalances and hierarchical arrangements, where certain individuals leverage their positions to exert undue influence or sabotage others. This dynamic fosters an atmosphere of apprehension and coercion, discouraging employees from voicing concerns or challenging the status quo for fear of reprisal. Also, toxic behaviors may extend beyond interpersonal interactions to encompass broader organizational practices, such as unfair expectations, lack of transparency, or discriminatory policies. These systemic issues perpetuate a culture of toxicity that pervades the entire organization, impacting morale, productivity, and overall welfare.

By cultivating heightened awareness of these patterns of toxicity, individuals can enhance their ability to identify and address these issues before they escalate. This entails not only observing individual behaviors but also scrutinizing the underlying structural and cultural factors contributing to toxicity in the workplace.

**Impact on Mental Health and Productivity**

The repercussions of toxicity in the workplace on mental health and productivity are deep and intricate, affecting every facet of our professional lives and more. Fundamentally, toxicity engenders an environment fraught with stress, apprehension, and ambiguity as individuals navigate through a labyrinth of interpersonal conflicts, power struggles, and adverse behaviors. The perpetual exposure to such deleterious elements can result in far-reaching consequences for our mental well-being, eroding our self-assurance, assurance, and sense of belonging within the organization.

Take, for instance, the toll of contending with an over controlling superior who scrutinizes every aspect of your work, leaving you feeling stifled and underappreciated. Or the exasperation of navigating office politics and cliques, where favoritism and betrayal undermine trust and cooperation. Compound that with the burden of encountering discrimination and harassment based on factors such as gender, race, or sexual orientation, and it's unsurprising that numerous employees find themselves grappling with feelings of isolation, inadequacy, and even despondency.

The cumulative impact of these stressors can materialize in a multitude of adverse mental health outcomes, spanning from burnout and anxiety to depression and even post-traumatic stress disorder (PTSD). The incessant pressure to perform, coupled with the apprehension of reprisal or retaliation for speaking out against toxic behavior, can ensnare individuals in a vortex of negativity and helplessness. Consequently, efficiency wanes as employees grapple to summon the motivation and concentration needed to excel in their roles. Instead of channeling their energies toward meaningful work and innovation, they find themselves expending invaluable resources navigating unsafe dynamics and safeguarding their mental and emotional well-being.

Likewise, the ramifications of toxicity extend beyond individual employees; they spread throughout the organization as a whole, impacting morale, engagement, and ultimately, the bottom line. Elevated levels of workplace stress and dissatisfaction can culminate in increased absenteeism, heightened turnover rates, and the exodus of talented employees seeking sanctuary in healthier work environments. This not only disrupts the continuity of business operations but also incurs significant costs associated with recruitment, training, and lost productivity.

Recognizing the interdependence of mental health and productivity underscores the urgency of addressing toxicity in the workplace and fostering a culture of respect, inclusivity, and support. By prioritizing employee well-being and cultivating environments where individuals feel valued, respected, and empowered to speak out against toxic behavior, organizations can unlock the full potential of their workforce and cultivate a thriving, sustainable workplace culture for years to come.

**Case Studies: Exemplifying Varied Forms of Workplace Toxicity**

**1. The Micromanagement Dilemma:** Emily, a dedicated project manager, found herself ensnared in an oppressive work environment where her every move was scrutinized by her supervisor. Despite Emily's extensive experience and proven track record of success, her superior insisted on dictating every detail of her work, leaving her feeling suffocated and undervalued. This incessant behavior eroded Emily's morale, ultimately resulting in burnout and a desire to depart from the company.

**2. The Toxic Team Atmosphere:** Alex, a skilled software developer, joined a new team only to discover the prevalence of toxic dynamics. Despite the team's technical prowess, communication was tainted with obnoxious and clique-like behavior. Alex found himself excluded from crucial discussions and decisions, as his colleagues favored individuals who aligned with their personal agendas. Attempts to rectify the situation were met with resistance and dismissal, exacerbating the toxic climate. Frustrated and disenchanted, Alex disengaged from his work, leading to a decline in performance and morale.

**3. The Culture of Intimidation**: A seasoned HR professional named Sarah, was employed by a company renowned for its cutthroat culture. From her first day, Sarah was subjected to relentless pressure to meet unattainable targets and adhere to rigid standards. Any deviation from the norm was met with swift reprimands and threats of termination. Witnessing colleagues being publicly admonished for minor errors created an atmosphere of fear and apprehension. Despite advocating for a more compassionate approach, Sarah faced opposition from senior leadership who prioritized outcomes over employee well-being. Feeling powerless to effect change, Sarah grappled with persistent stress and uncertainty about her future within the company.

**4. The Bullying Superior:** Jake, a young marketing associate, found himself in a hostile work environment where his supervisor routinely belittled and disparaged him in front of peers. Despite Jake's efforts to meet his supervisor's expectations and enhance his performance, the verbal abuse persisted. Jake's self-assurance plummeted, and he began to dread each day at work. Despite confiding in HR about the situation, Jake received minimal assistance or intervention, as the company culture tolerated and even normalized such behavior from senior leadership. Feeling entrapped and undervalued, Jake ultimately resigned from his position in pursuit of a healthier work milieu.

**5. The Discriminatory Custom:** Encountering discrimination and marginalization based on her gender in a predominantly male-dominated workplace was Maria, a talented graphic designer. Despite her innovative designs and contributions to the team, Maria's ideas were frequently disregarded or attributed to her male counterparts. She also endured inappropriate comments and conduct from male colleagues, fostering a hostile and unwelcoming ambiance. Despite raising concerns with HR, Maria received scant support or acknowledgment of the issue, as the company lacked the necessary policies and procedures to address gender discrimination effectively. Frustrated and demoralized, Maria left for a more inclusive workplace.

These instances illustrate the various forms of workplace toxicity and their negative impact on individuals and organizational culture. Addressing these issues is crucial for fostering an environment where all employees feel valued and respected.

# Chapter 2

## Responding to Dysfunction: Effective Strategies for Confrontation

When encountering toxicity at work, it's imperative to equip ourselves with effective approaches for tackling these issues directly. Whether it's managing a controlling superior, navigating office dynamics, or addressing discriminatory conduct, there are methods to safeguard our boundaries, preserve our well-being, and promote constructive change.

- **Transparent Dialogue:** Initiating open and sincere communication is a crucial initial step in addressing dysfunction.

Expressing concerns directly and respectfully to the involved parties encourages constructive dialogue, preventing underlying tensions from escalating.

- **Establishing Limits:** Clearly defining boundaries is vital for preserving mental and emotional health in toxic settings. Identifying acceptable and unacceptable behaviors and asserting ourselves when these boundaries are breached sends a clear message that mistreatment will not be tolerated.

- **Seeking Assistance:** Recognizing that we need not confront toxicity alone is key. Seeking guidance from trusted colleagues, mentors, or HR personnel offers valuable insights and support, validating our experiences and empowering us in our responses.

- **Documenting Instances:** In cases of severe or persistent toxicity, maintaining a record of incidents becomes necessary. This documentation can serve as evidence should formal action, such as lodging a complaint with HR or pursuing legal avenues, become necessary. Clear and factual documentation strengthens our case and illustrates the harmful behavioral patterns.

- **Pursuing Resolution:** Ultimately, the aim is to resolve dysfunction and foster positive change in the workplace. Engaging in mediation or conflict resolution processes facilitates dialogue and addresses underlying issues. Adopting a solution-focused approach and a willingness to collaborate can lead to constructive resolutions.

In summary, addressing workplace dysfunction demands assertiveness, effective communication, and resilience. By employing these strategies, we can confront toxicity head-on and advocate for a healthier and more conducive work environment for ourselves and our peers.

**Communication Techniques for Dealing with Toxic Behavior**

When handling toxic behavior at work, effective communication plays a pivotal role. By employing specific techniques, we can engage in challenging conversations with assurance and assertiveness, facilitating comprehension and encouraging positive transformations.

- **Utilize "I" Statements:** When addressing toxic behavior, it's crucial to express our concerns using "I" statements to convey our feelings about the situation. For instance, instead of stating, "You always micromanage me," we can say, "I feel overwhelmed and demotivated when I receive constant feedback on my work."

- **Focus on Specific Actions:** Rather than making broad accusations, it's beneficial to pinpoint particular behaviors causing distress. Providing concrete examples of the problematic conduct helps avoid misunderstandings and ensures clarity and actionable feedback.

- **Highlight Impact:** Illustrating the repercussions of toxic behavior on ourselves and others adds weight to our concerns. Whether detailing its impact on productivity, morale, or well-being, articulating tangible consequences aids in conveying the seriousness of the situation.

- **Practice Active Listening:** Effective communication entails active participation from both parties, necessitating attentive listening during discussions about toxic behavior. This involves giving undivided attention, summarizing their points for clarity, and acknowledging their emotions, even if we disagree with their viewpoint.

- **Explore Solutions:** Instead of fixating on negativity, focus on devising solutions and progressing collaboratively. Jointly brainstorming actionable steps to address toxic behavior showcases a commitment to resolving issues constructively.

- **Establish Boundaries:** Clearly articulating our boundaries and expectations regarding acceptable workplace behavior sets standards for how we wish to be treated and fosters accountability for maintaining a positive work environment.

- **Follow Through:** After addressing toxic behavior, it's essential to follow up with the individual to monitor progress. Acknowledge any positive changes and maintain open communication regarding any lingering concerns or challenges.

By incorporating these communication strategies, we can navigate discussions about unsafe behavior with confidence, empathy, and efficacy. Ultimately, fostering open dialogue and mutual respect is imperative for addressing toxicity and cultivating a healthier, more conducive work environment for all.

## Establishing Limits and Standing Up for Yourself

Setting and maintaining boundaries while asserting oneself confidently are pivotal steps in combatting detrimental behavior in professional environments. By clearly outlining acceptable and unacceptable conduct, individuals safeguard their integrity and promote a culture founded on respect and responsibility.

**1. Recognize Your Limits:** Reflect on the behaviors you're prepared to accept versus those that transgress your boundaries, encompassing verbal aggression, personal space violations, or excessive critique. Understanding these limits empowers individuals to assert themselves when necessary.

**2. Communicate Clearly:** Once boundaries are identified, communicate them assertively and respectfully to relevant parties. Clearly articulate unacceptable behavior and the repercussions for disregarding these boundaries. For instance, "I expect respectful communication. Any use of derogatory language or raised voices will result in termination of the conversation."

**3. Utilize Assertive Language:** Employ assertive language that exudes confidence and lucidity when stating your boundaries. Avoid apologizing or downplaying feelings, and instead, express yourself firmly and directly. For example, "I feel uneasy when interrupted during meetings. I anticipate uninterrupted speaking opportunities in the future."

**4. Remain Resolute:** It is common for others to challenge established boundaries, particularly if they're accustomed to overstepping without consequence. Maintain steadfastness and refuse to yield when faced with boundary-testing situations. Remember, assertiveness isn't about confrontation but about advocating for personal well-being and dignity.

**5. Implement Consequences**: In cases of repeated boundary violations despite clear communication, enforcing consequences is imperative. Options include removing oneself from the situation, seeking support from HR or a supervisor, or establishing firmer boundaries moving forward. Consistency underscores the seriousness of boundary enforcement.

**6. Prioritize Self-Care:** Establishing and upholding boundaries can be emotionally taxing, necessitating self-care measures to sustain well-being. Whether through breaks, engaging in enjoyable activities, or seeking support from loved ones, ensuring self-nurturance is essential amidst boundary assertion.

**7. Seek Assistance as Needed:** If struggling to assert boundaries or encountering resistance, don't hesitate to seek guidance from trusted peers, mentors, or HR. Having a supportive ally can offer valuable insights and encouragement during challenging circumstances.

By steadfastly setting and asserting boundaries, individuals lay the groundwork for healthier, more respectful workplace dynamics. Remember, advocating for personal well-being isn't just necessary; it's a fundamental entitlement as a valued team member.

## Finding Assistance: Allies and Resources for Managing Toxicity

In the often tumultuous terrain of the workplace, confronting toxicity can seem like traversing hazardous waters solo. However, it is essential to realize that you need not shoulder the burden alone. Seeking assistance from allies and making use of accessible resources can play a vital role in navigating and addressing toxic behavior effectively.

Primarily, identifying allies within your workplace can instill a sense of unity and empowerment. Trusted colleagues, mentors, or supervisors who comprehend your experiences and share your dedication to nurturing a healthier work environment can furnish invaluable guidance, insight, and support. Whether it involves confiding in a coworker during a coffee break or seeking mentorship from an experienced professional, having allies backing you can significantly enhance your ability to tackle toxicity confidently.

Moreover, establishing or joining support networks focused on addressing workplace toxicity can cultivate a sense of belonging and affirmation. Connecting with individuals who have encountered similar obstacles can provide a safe haven to exchange experiences, seek advice, and devise effective strategies. Whether through an informal coworker group or a formal professional network, these support systems can serve as pillars of strength and resilience amid adversity.

Additionally, leveraging the resources available within your organization can be indispensable in maneuvering through toxic dynamics. Many companies extend Employee Assistance Programs (EAPs) that furnish confidential counseling, resources, and aid for employees grappling with personal or professional hurdles. These programs proffer a non-judgmental space to discuss concerns, explore potential remedies, and access supplementary support services if required.

Engaging with your organization's HR department or employee relations team can also offer guidance and assistance in addressing workplace toxicity. HR professionals are adept at managing workplace issues and can provide support in navigating intricate dynamics, including avenues for mediation, conflict resolution, and lodging formal complaints if warranted. Do not hesitate to solicit help if you're contending with persistent or severe toxicity in the workplace – your HR team is there to assist you.

In certain instances, seeking external support from professional coaches, therapists, or legal advisors may be imperative to effectively address workplace toxicity. These experts can furnish specialized expertise and counsel tailored to your unique circumstances, aiding you in negotiating complex dynamics and advocating for your well-being with assurance.

Educating yourself about toxic behavior and effective strategies for addressing it can empower you to navigate challenging situations more adeptly. Avail yourself of resources such as literature, articles, workshops, and online courses focusing on workplace dynamics, communication proficiencies, and conflict resolution. Equipping yourself with knowledge and skills can fortify your confidence and resilience in confronting toxicity head-on.

Lastly, remember to prioritize self-care amidst the trials of addressing workplace toxicity. Dealing with toxic behavior can exact a toll on your mental and emotional well-being, so make self-care a priority. Whether through mindfulness practices, engaging in hobbies you relish, or seeking support from loved ones, ensure that you're nurturing yourself amid the hurdles you encounter.

To sum up, seeking assistance from allies and utilizing accessible resources is indispensable for effectively navigating and addressing workplace toxicity. Recall that you're not alone in grappling with these challenges, and there are individuals and resources at your disposal to support you every step of the way. By harnessing the power of support networks, tapping into available resources, and prioritizing self-care, you empower yourself to confront toxicity with resilience, confidence, and integrity.

# Chapter 3

## Regaining Authority: Taking Steps Towards a Healthier Workplace

In the presence of workplace toxicity, regaining authority becomes climacteric in developing a healthier and more supportive atmosphere. Through proactive measures aimed at addressing underlying issues and nurturing a positive culture, we can empower ourselves and our peers to excel both professionally and personally.

**1. Lead through Example:** As individuals, we wield the influence to shape the culture and energy within our workplace. By embodying values of respect, empathy, and inclusivity in our interactions, we set a positive precedent for our colleagues and contribute to a supportive and cooperative work environment. Whether it entails lending a sympathetic ear to a struggling coworker or championing diversity and inclusion efforts, every action holds the potential to effect change.

**2. Foster Open Communication:** Encourage transparent and candid connections among team members by establishing platforms for dialogue and feedback. Whether through regular team meetings, anonymous suggestion channels, or individual check-ins, fostering an environment of openness and trust can facilitate early issue identification and prevent conflicts from escalating. By offering a secure space for individuals to voice concerns and exchange viewpoints, we cultivate a sense of belonging and mutual regard within the workplace.

**3. Implement Clear Policies and Protocols:** Enforcing unambiguous policies and protocols for addressing toxic behavior communicates a firm stance against such conduct in the workplace. Ensure that employees are familiar with their rights and obligations, and provide training and support for effectively navigating challenging situations. By establishing a framework for addressing humiliation and imposing consequences for transgressions, we instill accountability and foster a culture of respect and professionalism.

**4. Invest in Education and Advancement:** Offer avenues for employees to enhance their communication prowess, conflict resolution aptitude, and emotional intelligence through educational and developmental initiatives. Equipping employees with the tools and resources to navigate workplace challenges effectively empowers them to assert themselves confidently, resolve conflicts constructively, and cultivate positive relationships with peers. By investing in the growth and advancement of our workforce, we nurture a culture of continual learning and enhancement that benefits all.

**5. Embrace Diversity and Inclusion:** Embrace the diverse viewpoints, backgrounds, and experiences within your workforce by celebrating diversity and fostering inclusion. Create opportunities for employees to share their unique perspectives and contributions, ensuring that each individual feels valued and respected. By fostering a culture of inclusivity where all voices are heard and appreciated, we foster a more innovative, engaged, and harmonious workplace conducive to everyone's success.

**6. Assess and Review Progress:** Regularly evaluate the efficacy of initiatives aimed at addressing toxicity and cultivating a healthier workplace culture. Seek feedback from employees through surveys, focus groups, or informal conversations to gauge the impact of interventions and identify areas for refinement. By remaining attentive and responsive to the evolving needs of our workforce, we ensure that endeavors to regain control are substantive and sustainable in the long haul.

Through proactive measures aimed at regaining authority and fostering a healthier workplace, we establish an environment where every employee feels valued, respected, and empowered to thrive. Change is a gradual process that demands dedication and effort, but by uniting efforts and committing to a shared vision of inclusivity and respect, we can foster a workplace culture conducive to the success of all.

## Cultivating Resilience: Coping Mechanisms for Managing Toxicity

In our modern world, navigating through various forms of toxicity has become an essential skill for maintaining mental and emotional well-being. Cultivating resilience is crucial in this endeavor, as it equips individuals with coping mechanisms to effectively manage the challenges posed by these unsafe environments.

One key aspect of building resilience is developing a strong sense of self-awareness. By understanding our own triggers and vulnerabilities, we can better prepare ourselves to face toxic situations without being overwhelmed.

Fostering a concerned and encouraging network of relationships is another way of significantly bolstering our resilience against toxicity. Whether venting frustrations, seeking guidance, or having someone listen empathetically, support from others alleviates isolation and empowers us to confront adversity with resilience. Surrounding ourselves with people who uplift and validate our experiences provides a buffer against the negative effects of these pernicious conditions.

Furthermore, engaging in self-indulgent practices stands as a cornerstone of cultivating resilience. Amid the chaos of toxicity, neglecting our physical, emotional, and mental health is common. However, deliberately caring for ourselves is essential for replenishing our energy and sustaining persistence. This may entail incorporating activities like exercise, meditation, journaling, or spending time with loved ones into our routines. By doing this, we fortify ourselves against the corrosive effects of toxicity and empower ourselves to lead fulfilling lives despite the challenges we may encounter.

Setting healthy boundaries is another crucial aspect of resilience in the face of workplace toxicity. Clear boundaries safeguard our well-being and enable us to assert ourselves confidently when necessary. Whether it's refusing unreasonable demands or limiting engagement in toxic interactions, boundary-setting empowers us to prioritize our needs and values. Asserting boundaries signals to others that we won't tolerate mistreatment, preserving our dignity and self-worth.

Additionally, mindfulness practices can aid in managing stress and nurturing resilience amidst workplace toxicity. Techniques like deep breathing and meditation cultivate presence and clarity, enabling us to respond to challenges calmly. Mindfulness fosters self-awareness and emotional regulation, facilitating navigation of toxic environments with ease.

Moreover, focusing on what we control empowers us to address toxicity and enact positive change. While we can't control others' behavior or organizational culture, we influence our attitudes, behaviors, and responses. Advocating for needs, promoting open communication, and fostering inclusivity reclaim agency and empowerment in toxic environments.

## Advocating for Change: Initiating Dialogues and Actions for Improvement

This is a collaborative endeavor requiring courage, perseverance, and a dedication to cultivating a healthier and more supportive work environment. One pivotal step in addressing this is initiating discussions with relevant stakeholders regarding prevailing issues. This may involve speaking up in meetings, engaging in one-on-one conversations with supervisors, or facilitating group dialogues to collectively address concerns. By articulating experiences and grievances constructively and respectfully, we raise awareness and lay the groundwork for positive change.

Promoting change often necessitates gathering evidence and data to substantiate our claims. Documenting instances of toxicity, soliciting feedback from peers, and researching effective strategies for tackling workplace issues strengthens our arguments and underscore the imperative for intervention. By presenting factual evidence and tangible examples, we make a compelling case for the urgency and necessity of change.

Engaging in collective action is another potent means of advocating for transformation and effecting tangible improvements in the workplace. This may entail forging alliances with like-minded colleagues to amplify our voices, orchestrating petitions or advocacy campaigns to spotlight specific issues, or participating in employee-driven initiatives aimed at cultivating a healthier organizational culture. By mobilizing collective efforts, we harness the strength of unity and demonstrate solidarity in our commitment to positive change.

In addition to initiating discussions and taking collective action, advocating for transformation demands persistence and resilience in the face of resistance or setbacks. Change often encounters opposition, whether from individuals entrenched in the status quo or institutional obstacles perpetuating toxic norms. Nonetheless, by remaining steadfast in our convictions and persisting in our advocacy efforts, we dismantle barriers to progress and pave the path toward a brighter future.

Proposing tangible solutions and alternatives to address the root causes of toxicity is another perspective for upholding change. This may involve implementing new policies and protocols to prevent and address misconduct, providing training and resources to foster diversity and inclusivity, or nurturing a culture of accountability and respect through leadership development initiatives. By offering actionable recommendations for enhancement, we demonstrate our commitment to finding sustainable solutions beneficial to all.

## Legal Considerations: Grasping Rights and Recourse Options

Maneuvering toxicity in the workplace can be emotionally and mentally taxing, but it's crucial to recognize that avenues for rights and recourse exist. Understanding the legal aspects surrounding workplace toxicity is vital for safeguarding yourself and advocating for positive change.

Primarily, acquaint yourself with the laws and regulations governing workplace conduct and safeguards against harassment, discrimination, and retaliation. These may encompass federal statutes like Title VII of the Civil Rights Act, the

Americans with Disabilities Act (ADA), the Age Discrimination in Employment Act (ADEA), and the Occupational Safety and Health Act (OSHA), along with state and local provisions offering further protections.

In the event you believe you've faced harassment, discrimination, or retaliation at work, it's imperative to document incidents and gather evidence substantiating your claims. This could entail maintaining a comprehensive log detailing dates, times, and descriptions of problematic conduct, as well as amassing any pertinent correspondence, messages, or records corroborating your experiences.

Once evidence is compiled, contemplate seeking assistance from HR, a supervisor, or an employment law attorney to explore potential avenues for recourse. Depending on the severity and nature of the misconduct, you might pursue a formal complaint with HR or a government body like the Equal Employment Opportunity Commission (EEOC) or the Department of Labor (DOL), or initiate legal proceedings through a civil lawsuit.

Before proceeding formally, it's crucial to weigh the potential risks and repercussions, as well as the likelihood of a favorable outcome. Legal processes can be protracted, emotionally taxing, and may strain workplace relationships, necessitating careful consideration of options and guidance from knowledgeable professionals.

In addition to legal recourse, contemplate alternative methods for resolving workplace conflicts and addressing toxicity, such as mediation or arbitration, wherein a neutral third party facilitates discussions to reach a mutually agreeable resolution. These alternative dispute resolution mechanisms are often quicker, less adversarial, and more conducive to preserving working relationships than traditional litigation.

Ultimately, grasping your rights and recourse options enables you to assert control over your circumstances and advocate for a healthier, more respectful workplace. Whether through informal dialogue with HR, mediation, or legal action, recognize your ability to combat workplace toxicity and seek justice for yourself and others. By asserting your rights and holding those engaging in harmful behavior accountable, you contribute to fostering a workplace culture founded on respect, fairness, and equality for all.

# Chapter 4

## Promoting Positive Transformation: Building a Healthy Work Environment

Developing a nurturing work atmosphere transcends merely tackling toxicity; it involves nurturing a background marked by respect, inclusivity, and encouragement, wherein every employee can flourish. Advancing positive transformation demands a concerted endeavor from individuals, leaders, and organizations to nurture a workplace ethos that prizes well-being, cooperation, and advancement.

Individuals hold a critical role in propelling positive transformation within their organizations. By embodying virtues like respect, concern, and sensitivity in their interactions with peers, individuals can contribute to a milieu of mutual regard and collaboration. This encompasses speaking out against toxic conduct, bolstering colleagues facing adversities, and championing inclusive norms and policies.

Also, organizations must institute systemic measures to foster positive transformation and cultivate a nurturing work atmosphere for all employees. This encompasses implementing policies and protocols that address toxic conduct, such as stringent prohibitions against harassment and discrimination, clear channels for lodging and redressing grievances, and regular education on themes like diversity, equity, and inclusion. Moreover, they can also invest in initiatives and schemes that boost employee well-being, including employee assistance programs, mental health support resources, and endeavors to encourage work-life equilibrium. By prioritizing the holistic well-being of their workforce, organizations can engender a culture characterized by trust, resilience, and engagement, yielding favorable outcomes for individuals and the organization at large.

**The Role of Leadership in Addressing and Preempting Workplace Toxicity**

The mantle of leadership is heavily laden with the duty to manage and preempt toxicity within the workplace. As architects of the company's culture, leaders possess the clout to shape the standards, values, and behaviors that define the corporate environment. The impetus for positive change is primarily driven by leadership. They hold a figurative sway in crafting the company's moral fiber and demonstrating the conduct they wish to be mirrored by their team.

Moreover, leaders are tasked with placing the well-being of their team at the forefront by nurturing clear communication, paving pathways for career advancement, and fostering an environment of support. This involves attentively listening to employee input, swiftly tackling issues that arise, and championing policies and practices that promote a balance between professional and personal life, as well as mental health.

Leaders also have the responsibility to lead by example in maintaining a secure and friendly workplace atmosphere. This includes displaying honesty, empathy, and fairness in dealings with employees and colleagues alike. Leaders who practice respectful and inclusive behavior set a standard for the entire company, demonstrating a zero-tolerance stance on toxic actions and reinforcing the respect and value of every team member.

In addition, leaders are expected to invest in educational and growth-focused initiatives that advocate for constructive workplace behavior and foster a culture of respect and inclusivity. This includes providing training in areas such as effective communication, conflict management, awareness of unconscious biases, and principles of diversity, equity, and inclusion.

Beyond merely addressing present toxicity, leaders are also charged with taking proactive steps to prevent such issues from arising. This entails setting clear standards and expectations for behavior, implementing rules and procedures that prohibit harassment and discrimination, and cultivating an environment where employees feel confident to express any concerns they might face.

**Strategies for Revitalizing Workplace Environments to Foster Teamwork and Excellence**

Establishing a thriving and affirmative work atmosphere is crucial for the well-being of staff and the prosperity of the company. Confronting a detrimental organizational culture necessitates the adoption of potent strategies for a positive overhaul. Below are strategies to convert a negative environment into a supportive and top-performing culture:

**1. Enhanced Communication Practices:**

   - Promote a culture of openness in communication across all echelons. It's vital that staff members are at ease when voicing their concerns, sharing ideas, and offering feedback.

   - Cultivate a culture of attentive listening within the workforce and among the leadership. Frequent updates, community forums, and confidential feedback mechanisms can aid in this endeavor.

## 2. Exemplary Leadership:

- The influence of leadership in molding the company's culture is pivotal. They must personify the conduct they wish to see in their team.

- Display compassion, dignity, and impartiality. A leadership that values the welfare of its employees establishes a commendable organizational tone.

## 3. Effective Dispute Management:

- Tackle disputes swiftly and positively. Equip supervisors and staff with dispute resolution skills.

- Promote a spirit of cooperation and mutual concession. In times of conflict, the focus should be on devising solutions instead of pointing fingers.

**4. Fostering a Safe Space for Innovation:**

- Forge an environment where taking calculated risks, proposing novel concepts, and acknowledging errors is safe.

- Applaud educational moments and developmental strides over penalizing setbacks.

**5. Acknowledgment and Gratitude:**

- Consistently express gratitude for the hard work of employees. Acknowledge accomplishments, whether they are significant or minor.

- Such recognition can lift spirits and encourage the continuation of positive actions.

**6. Ongoing Education and Advancement:**

- Commit to perpetual education and enhancement of skills. Offer avenues for staff to advance their competencies.

- Educational initiatives can bolster performance and satisfaction at work, leading to a culture of high achievement.

**7. Defining Roles and Ambitions:**

- Establish transparent benchmarks for performance and objectives. It's important that employees grasp their duties and what is expected of them.

- Periodically assess progress and offer constructive critique. Ensure personal ambitions are in harmony with the company's vision.

**8. Encouraging Equilibrium Between Work and Life:**

- Support a balanced approach to professional and personal life. Refrain from burdening staff with undue workloads.

- Adaptable working conditions, health initiatives, and psychological support can foster a more agreeable work climate.

**9. Eradicating Intimidation and Prejudice:**

- Formulate stringent regulations against intimidation, bias, and harassment in the workplace.

- Promptly look into grievances and implement suitable measures to uphold a courteous atmosphere.

**10. Embracing and Valuing Diversity:**

- Welcome the full spectrum of diversity. Develop a culture of inclusivity where every individual feels esteemed and integral.

- Appreciate the distinct advantages that diverse experiences and viewpoints contribute to the enterprise.

It is important to note that the evolution of workplace culture is a gradual process that demands unwavering dedication. By putting these strategies into practice, companies can forge an environment conducive to employee engagement, cooperative efforts, and peak performance.

**Maintaining Momentum: Ensuring Long-Term Viability of a Positive Work Environment**

The cultivation of a vibrant workplace culture is a key element in the tapestry of organizational achievement. Such a culture nurtures employee commitment, efficiency, and well-being. The endeavor to instill this culture is not a fleeting task but a perpetual commitment that demands thoughtful action. This discourse delves into the methodologies required to maintain momentum and safeguard a nurturing workplace culture for the foreseeable future.

**1. Ongoing Assessment and Modification**

The longevity of a culture conducive to productivity hinges on the regular appraisal of its vitality. Utilizing employee surveys, feedback channels, and performance indicators, organizations can monitor the pulse of their cultural health. Adaptability is the hallmark of a resilient culture, allowing for recalibration in response to internal growth and external shifts.

## 2. Unwavering Emphasis on Foundational Principles

An organization's foundational principles are the compass by which its culture is navigated. These principles must be articulated with clarity and woven into the fabric of the organization's daily existence. Through consistent reinforcement—manifested in company narratives, collective gatherings, and accolades—these principles become ingrained in the organizational psyche.

## 3. Dedication from the Helm

The echelons of leadership are instrumental in sculpting the cultural landscape. Their unwavering dedication to the culture's embodiment is non-negotiable. Training for leaders should encompass the nurturing of a supportive atmosphere as much as the honing of strategic acumen. Leadership that champions the cause of employee prosperity sets a commendable precedent.

**4. Inclusive Participation and Empowerment**

Employee participation in shaping the culture engenders a sense of belonging and empowerment. The formation of committees or groups dedicated to cultural matters allows for grassroots involvement in cultural stewardship. When individuals are vested with cultural ownership, they become the vanguard of positive transformation.

**5. Advocating a Progressive Mindset**

A progressive mindset is the cornerstone of a culture that values enhancement. Organizations should establish avenues for the free flow of ideas and ingenuity. Whether it's through open forums, collaborative sessions, or interdisciplinary teams, a culture that prizes progress ensures its own dynamism.

## 6. Comprehensive Integration and Education

The cultural initiation of newcomers should commence from the outset. Onboarding processes that transcend technical orientation to impart cultural values set the stage for alignment. Periodic educational sessions for all personnel serve to refresh these values and facilitate personal and professional growth.

## 7. Clarity and Equity in Governance

Clarity in governance fosters trust among the workforce. Employees should be well-versed in organizational regulations and their equitable application. The periodic reassessment of policies ensures they remain in sync with the cultural aspirations and ethical standards of the organization.

## 8. Visionary Cultural Foresight

A visionary approach to cultural development is essential. This foresight should resonate with the strategic aspirations of the organization. By sharing this vision with all employees, it becomes an integral part of the decision-making process and a guiding light for future endeavors.

# Conclusion

In our endeavor to address and transform toxic workplace cultures into supportive and productive ones, we have examined a variety of strategies and principles crucial for achieving success. Ranging from leadership commitment to ongoing assessment, effective communication, and the promotion of inclusivity and diversity, each element plays a pivotal role in nurturing a healthy work environment conducive to employee flourishing.

It is evident that constructing and sustaining a healthy workplace culture is not a singular endeavor but rather a continuous voyage demanding dedication, attentiveness, and adaptability. Through prioritizing leadership commitment, continual assessment, effective communication, training and development, fostering inclusivity and diversity, recognizing and rewarding positive behaviors, and perpetually striving for improvement, organizations can establish environments where employees are esteemed, respected, and empowered to realize their full potential.

As we progress, let us recall that the task of building and sustaining a healthy workplace culture is a shared obligation necessitating the collective endeavor of leaders, employees, and organizations. Through collaborative efforts, we can forge workplaces devoid of toxicity, where everyone feels supported, engaged, and capable of thriving.

Finally, let us remain steadfast in nurturing cultures of respect, inclusivity, and collaboration, wherein every individual is valued and empowered to contribute their unique skills and perspectives. Together, we can cultivate workplaces that not only propel organizational success but also enrich the lives of all who partake in them.

www.ingramcontent.com/pod-product-compliance
Lightning Source LLC
Chambersburg PA
CBHW050236230526
45470CB00005B/1972